KW-222-528

Microsoft®
WORD 97

ENI Publishing LTD

500 Chiswick High Road
London W4 5RG

Tel : 0181 956 23 20
Fax : 0181 956 23 21

e-mail: publishing@ediENI.com
http://www.editions-eni.com

Editions ENI

BP 32125
44021 NANTES Cedex 1

Tel. 33.2.40.92.45.45
Fax 33.2.40.92.45.46

e-mail : editions@ediENI.com
http://www.editions-eni.com

Straight to the point collection directed by Corinne HERVO
This edition by Françoise BRETAGNE
Translated from the French by Gillian CAIN

Foreword

The aim of this book is to let you find rapidly how to perform any task in **Microsoft Word 97**.

Each procedure is described in detail and illustrated so that you can put it into action easily.

The final pages are given over to an **index** of the topics covered and an **appendix**, which gives details of shortcut keys.

The typographic conventions used in this book are as follows:

Type faces used for specific purposes:	
bold	indicates the option to take in a menu or dialog box.
italic	is used for notes and comments.
Ctrl	represents a key from the keyboard; when two keys appear side by side, they should be pressed simultaneously.

Symbols indicating the content of a paragraph:	
▓	an action to carry out (activating an option, clicking with the mouse...).
⇨	a general comment on the command in question.
↷🖰	a technique which involves the mouse.
⬙	a keyboard technique.
📄	a technique which uses options from the menus.

▣ OVERVIEW

▣ TEXT

▣ PRINTING OPTIONS

▣ FORMATTING

▣ DRAWING

▣ TEMPLATES

🔲 FINDING/REPLACING TEXT

🔲 NOTES AND BOOKMARKS

🔲 TABLES/CHARTS

🔲 FORMS/MAIL MERGES

🔲 MACROS

APPENDIX

INDEX

1.1 The environment

A-Starting/Leaving Microsoft Word 97

- Click the **Start** button.
- Open the **Programs** menu then click the **Microsoft Word** option.
- To leave Word,

File	Click ☒ in the	Alt F4
Exit	application window	

B-Presenting the workscreen

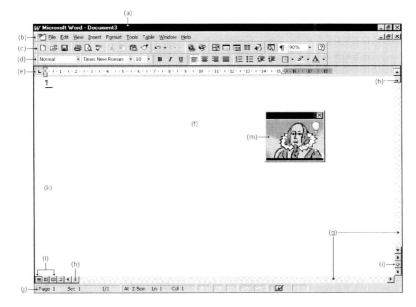

(a) the **title bar and icons** with the button which displays the application's Control menu (W), the buttons for managing the application window, the application's name and the name of the current document.

(b) the **menu bar**: on the left, the button which displays the document's Control menu ( ) and the names of the menus available in Word.

(c) (d) the **Standard toolbar** and the **Formatting toolbar**: if they are not visible on your screen, activate the appropriate options in the **View - Toolbars** menu.

(e)	the **horizontal ruler**: to see the ruler on the screen, activate the option in the **View** menu or press [Alt] [⇧ Shift] **R**.
(f)	the **workspace**.
(g) (h)	the **scroll bar** and **cursors**: drag the cursor or click the arrows to scroll through the document.
(i)	the **Select Browse Object button**: click this button to move around a document.
(j)	the **status bar**.
(k)	the **selection bar**.
(l)	the **view buttons**.
(m)	the **Office Assistant** displays tips and help texts relevant to the task in progress.

C-Dialog boxes

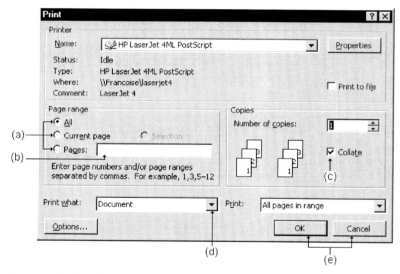

(a)	**Option buttons**: the active option is marked with a black dot.
(b)	**Text boxes**.
(c)	**Check boxes**: the option is active when the box is checked.
(d)	**List boxes**: to see the list, click the down arrow.
(e)	**Command buttons**: the **OK** button executes your command and closes the dialog box ([Enter]), the **Cancel** button negates the command and closes the dialog box ([Esc]).

*In many dialog boxes, related options are grouped together under separate **tabs**.*

tabs

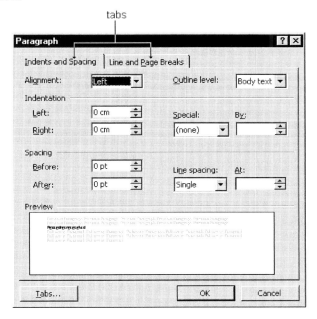

D-Undoing your last action(s)

Undoing one action

Edit
Undo

Ctrl Z

Undoing several actions

Open the list by clicking the down arrow on the button.

Click the last of the actions you wish to cancel (this action, and everything you have done since, will be undone).

Use the redo button to redo what you have cancelled.

E-Repeating your last action

▓ Edit - Redo or [F4] (or [Ctrl] Y)

F-Using the Office Assistant

▓ If the Office Assistant is not displayed, click [?].
▓ Click the Office Assistant when you need help with the job in progress.

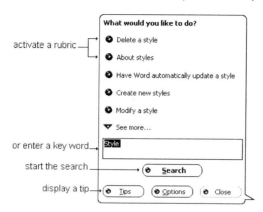

A light bulb in the Office Assistant indicates that Word has a tip for you. Click the Assistant to read the tip.

▓ To change the Office Assistant's look, click the **Options** button in the Office Assistant window then activate the **Gallery** tab.

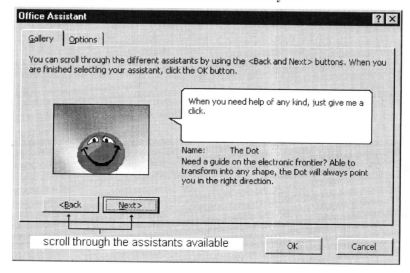

1.2 Viewing the content of the window

A-Showing/hiding nonprinting characters

When these characters are visible, it is easy to see spaces, ends of paragraphs...

Click ¶ or press [Ctrl] [⇧ Shift] * to display (or hide) the nonprinting characters.

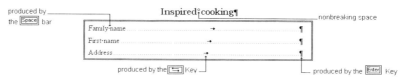

B-Choosing the zoom

View - Zoom...

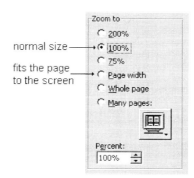

↪ *You can also use the list box on the far right of the* **Standard** *toolbar.*

C-Changing the view

There are three views to choose from:

View
Normal

This view shows the text with its formatting, but simplifies the page layout.

View
Online Layout

Document Map →

The Mongol Campaign in E
Background
Organisation
Russian lands
Hungary
Poland
Kahn of Kahns
The Great Khans
Great Khans After Ogodei

The Mongol Campaign in Europe

Background

*All empires from sunrise to sunset have
been given to us, and we own them.*
— GUYUK, THIRD GREAT KHAN OF THE MONGOLS

TO EUROPEANS of the 13th century they were the horde
from hell. Tartars from Tartarus, that part of Hades
where the wicked were punished. They had the heads
of dogs, and they devoured the bodies of their victims.
Indeed, the Tartars, as Europeans called the Mongols,
sometimes did eat the raw hearts or livers of slain foes, hoping
to capture their spirits. Europeans knew little about these

Page 1   Sec 1   1/22   At 0cm   Ln   Col 1

This view incorporates the Document Map.

▦ **View**
Page Layout

*This view shows the document as it will be printed, with its formatting and
page layout (columns, margins...).*

1.3 Documents

A-Opening a document

▦ **File**
Open   ⌨ O

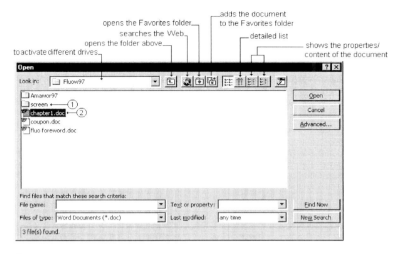

to activate different drives — opens the folder above — searches the Web — opens the Favorites folder — adds the document to the Favorites folder — detailed list — shows the properties/content of the document

① Open the folder containing the document by double-clicking its icon.

② Double-click the name of the document.

⇨ *By holding down* ⇧ Shift *or* Ctrl*, you can select several documents to open at once.*

B-Closing a document

▓ File Close	Click ☒ in the document window	Ctrl W or Ctrl F4

⇨ *To close all open documents, hold the* ⇧ Shift *key down, open the* **File** *menu, then click* **Close All***.*

C-Creating a new document

▓ File New OK	◻	Ctrl N

⇨ *If you would like a Wizard to guide you through the creation of a new document, pick one of the* **Wizard** *templates available in the* **New** *dialog box.*

D-Saving a document

A new document

▓ File Save		Ctrl S

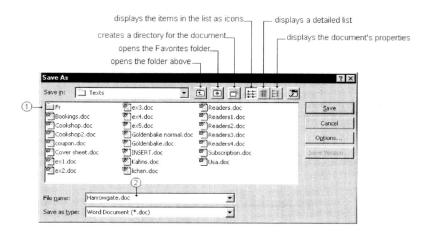

displays the items in the list as icons — displays a detailed list
creates a directory for the document — displays the document's properties
opens the Favorites folder
opens the folder above

① Open the folder where you want to store the document by double-clicking its icon.

② Give a name for the document (up to 255 characters, including spaces).

An existing document

File
Save

⬛ [Ctrl] S

⇨ *Word has an automatic "AutoRecover" save function which you can activate or deactivate in the* **Tools - Options** *dialog box, under the* **Save** *tab.*

⇨ *To save all open documents, hold down the* [⇧ Shift] *key as you open the* **File** *menu, then click* **Save All**.

⇨ *To create backup copies (extension .BAK), activate the* **Always create backup copy** *option in* **Tools - Options, Save** *tab.*

E- Activating a document which is open but hidden

⬛ Open the **Window** menu.

⬛ On the keyboard, [Ctrl][⇧ Shift][F6] activates the document before the current document, and [Ctrl][F6] the one after.

⇨ *To see all the open documents on the screen at the same time, use the command* **Window - Arrange All**.

F- Inserting a document inside another

⬛ Position the insertion point where you want to insert the document, then use **Insert - File...**

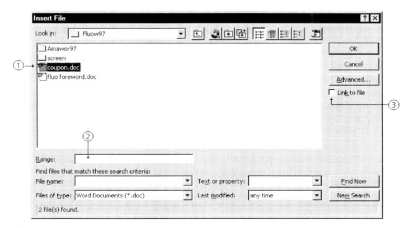

① Select the document to be inserted.

② If appropriate, specify the name of a bookmark or a range which corresponds to the part of the file you wish to insert.

③ Check the box if you want to create a link between the documents.

G-Using passwords to protect a document

▪ **File - Save** or **Save As...**

▪ Click the **Options** button.

▪ Give a **Password to open** and/or a **Password to modify** (you are limited to 15 characters: as you type, the characters are replaced by asterisks).

▪ Type the same password(s) again then click the **OK** button.

▪ Click **Save**.

H-Searching for a document

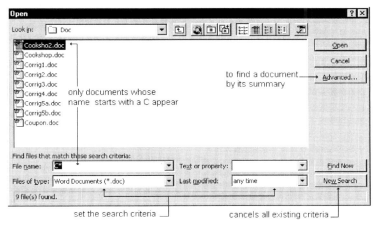

I- Creating a summary of the properties of a document

Give the title, the subject of the document, the name of the author... it will be easier to find your document if you forget its name.

In the **Open** dialog box, select the document concerned, click 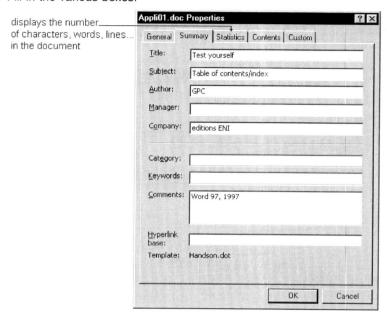 then click **Properties**.

Fill in the various boxes:

displays the number of characters, words, lines... in the document

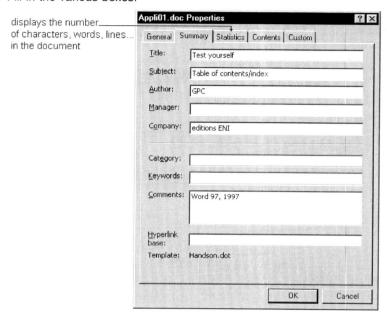

⇨ *To remind yourself to fill in the properties of every new document you create, go into the **Tools - Options** dialog box, click the **Save** tab, then activate the choice **Prompt for document properties**.*

J- Saving different versions of the same document

A version is a "snapshot" of your document at a particular moment. The various versions of a document are stored in the document : no new file is created.

Go into the document concerned.

File - Versions

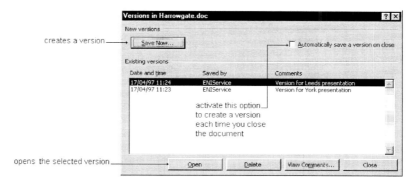

creates a version ⟶

activate this option
to create a version
each time you close
the document

opens the selected version ⟶

- To create a version, click the **Save Now** button and enter a comment which identifies it.

⇨ *To save a version as a document in its own right, open it and use the File - Save As command.*

1.4 The configuration

A-Activating/deactivating the AutoFormat function

- **Tools - AutoCorrect**
AutoFormat As You Type tab

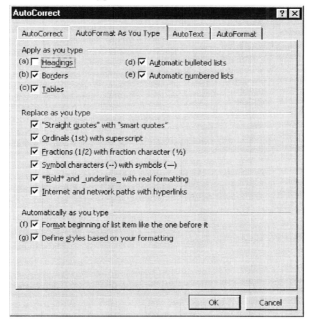

(a) once the option is active, if you press ⌷Enter⌷ once at the beginning of a paragraph and twice at the end of a paragraph, then that paragraph will be put into the style **Heading 1**. If you press ⌷Enter⌷ then the ⌷⇄⌷ key at the beginning of your paragraph and ⌷Enter⌷ twice at the end, it will be put into the **Heading 2** style.

(b) once the option is active, if you type three consecutive hyphens (---) then ⌷Enter⌷ at the beginning of a paragraph, then that paragraph will be underlined with a single line. If you type three consecutive equal signs (===) then ⌷Enter⌷, the following paragraph will be underlined with a double line.

(c) once the option is active, if you type +--+--+, a table is created with one column for every pair of + signs (in this example: 2 columns).

(d) once this option is active, if you begin a paragraph with an asterisk, the letter O, the > sign or a dash followed by a space or a tab, then the beginning of that paragraph, and successive ones, will be marked with a bullet.

(e) once the option is active, if you begin a paragraph with a number or letter followed by a full stop, and a space or tab, then that paragraph and successive ones will be numbered.

(f) if this option is active, and (for example) the first word in a list is in bold type, word applies bold type to the first word of the next item in the list.

(g) if this option is active, Word creates new styles incorporating the formatting you have done manually.

B-Displaying an extra toolbar

▓ **View - Toolbars** or right-click one of the toolbars.
▓ Check the bar(s) you wish to display.

C-Moving a toolbar

▓ Double-click the move handle (the double line at the very left of the toolbar) or point this handle and drag: the bar becomes a "floating" toolbar.
▓ To dock the floating bar, double-click its title bar or drag it to an edge of the workspace.

D-Customising a toolbar

- Go into the template concerned.
- **View** - **Toolbars** - **Customize**

Removing a tool

- If necessary, click the **Toolbars** tab.
- On the toolbar itself, click the tool you wish to remove, and drag it off the bar.

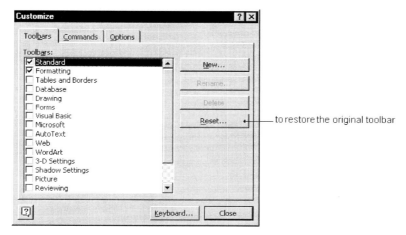

to restore the original toolbar

Adding a tool

- Click the **Commands** tab.

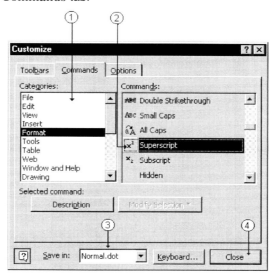

① Select the category of the tool.

② Select the tool then drag the button directly onto the toolbar itself (in the Word window).

③ Select the right template.

④ Close the dialog box.

Creating a custom toolbar

▒ Under the **Toolbars** tab, click **New**.

▒ Enter a name for the toolbar you wish to create in **Toolbar name**.

▒ Choose the template concerned in the **Make toolbar available to** list.

▒ Enter.

▒ Add the tools you require then dock the toolbar by double-clicking its title.

2.1 Moving around and selecting

A-Moving the insertion point

Use the following keys to move the insertion point around:

→/←	Next/previous character
Ctrl → /Ctrl ←	Beginning of next/previous word
End /Home	End/beginning of the line
Ctrl ↓ /Ctrl ↑	Beginning of the next/previous paragraph
Alt Pg Dn /Ctrl Alt Pg Up	Bottom/top of the window
Pg Dn /Pg Up	Next/previous window
Ctrl Home /Ctrl End	Beginning/end of the document.

Use the scroll bars:

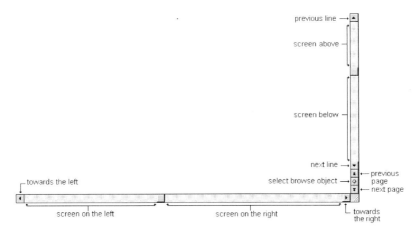

To go straight to a point in the document, drag the scroll cursor along the scroll bar to that point's approximate position then click the insertion point into place.

To move from object to object (headings, sections...) in a document, click the button ⊙ then click the button representing the type of object which interests you. Use the **Next** button (Ctrl Pg Dn) and/or the **Previous** button (Ctrl Pg Up): these buttons with blue arrows replace the **Next page** and **Previous Page** buttons.

B-Using the Document Map

■ View
   Document Map

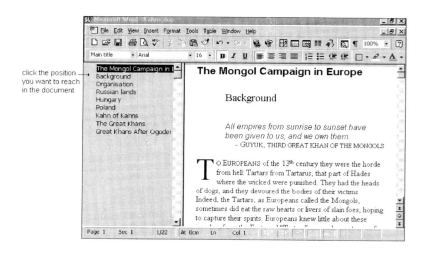

click the position
you want to reach
in the document

■ Click 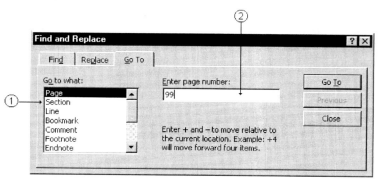 to deactivate the Document Map.

C-Going to a specific object in a document

■ **Edit - Go To** or ⌐Ctrl⌐ **G** (or double-click the **Page** information on the status bar).

① Specify what it is you wish to move to
② Enter its number.

↪ *Enter 50% to go to the middle of the document.*

⇨ *You can put several instructions together: for example, P4L10 will take you to line 10 of page 4.*

D-Selecting text

Selecting part of the text

	A word	double-click the word.
	a line	point just to the left of the line and click once.
	a paragraph	point just to the left of the paragraph and double-click.
	a sentence	point to the sentence, hold down the Ctrl button and click once.
	a group of characters	drag over all the characters concerned or click in front of the first character, hold down the ⇧ Shift key and click just after the last.

Position the insertion point before the first character and hold down the ⇧ Shift key as you use the direction keys to select,

or,

position the insertion point in the text you wish to select then press F8 (**EXT** appears in black on the status bar: the extension of selection mode is activated). Press F8 a second, third, fourth, fifth or sixth time to select the word, the sentence, the paragraph, the section or the whole document. Press Esc to come out of extension mode.

⇨ *Once the indicator EXT appears in black on the status bar, you can extend the selection by typing in the last letter you wish to select. For example, if you press Enter, the selection is extended to the end of the paragraph.*

⇨ *To select columns of text, hold the Alt key down as you drag.*

Selecting an entire document

Edit - Select All (Ctrl A) or point the left edge of the text, hold down the Ctrl button and click once (or triple-click the left edge of the text).

2.2 Entering and modifying text

A-Entering text

Position the insertion point where you wish to enter the text. Type the text: Word takes care of the line breaks. Press enter to start a new para-graph and use the following keys:

⇧ Shift Enter	manual line break
Ctrl Enter	manual page break
⇄	to move to the next tab stop.

Microsoft Word 97

To enter formatted text, activate the attribute(s) you wish to apply, type in the text then cancel the attribute.

When you enter the first characters of today's date, a day of the week, a month, a Screen Tip appears displaying the full expression (if the option **Show AutoComplete tip for AutoText and dates** is active in the **Auto-Text** dialog box). Press ⌈Enter⌋ if you want to accept Word's suggestion; otherwise continue typing.

B-Deleting text

⌈←⌋/⌈Del⌋   to delete the previous character or the following character.

⌈Ctrl⌋⌈←⌋/⌈Ctrl⌋⌈Del⌋   to delete the beginning/end of the current word.

C-Leaving/activating insert mode

Double-click the **OVR** indicator on the status bar (in overtype mode, the characters you type replace the existing ones).

D-Changing between upper and lower case characters

Select the text, then **Format - Change Case...**

Double-click the case you want to apply.

⇨ *The shortcut key* ⌈û Shift⌋⌈F3⌋ *puts the text first into upper case, then into lower case, then into title case.*

E-Inserting special text

Nonbreaking hyphens/spaces

⌈Ctrl⌋_   nonbreaking hyphen

⌈Ctrl⌋⌈û Shift⌋⌈space⌋   nonbreaking space.

A date

Position the insertion point and press ⌈Alt⌋⌈û Shift⌋ **D**.

Insert - Date and Time

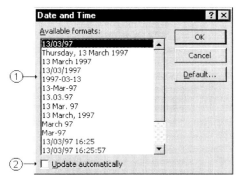

① Click the format you prefer.

② If you want the date printed in your document to be updated automatically, activate this check box.

Symbols

Insert - Symbol...
Symbols tab

to zoom in on a symbol click it

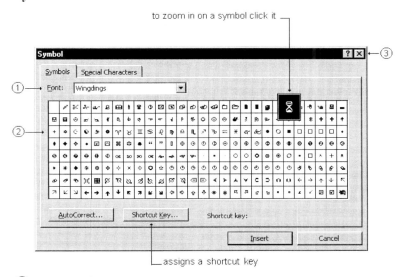

assigns a shortcut key

① Select the font.

② Double-click the character to insert.

③ Shut the dialog box.

⇨ *To associate a shortcut key with a symbol, click **Shortcut Key**, give the shortcut key, click **Assign** then **Close**.*

F-Making a break between sections

Position the insertion point then **Insert - Break**.

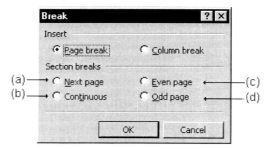

(a)	a page break between sections.
(b)	the new section begins straight after the previous one.
(c)/(d)	Word will start to print the new section on the next even-numbered/odd-numbered page.

G-Moving/copying part of a text

Using the clipboard

Select the text.

To move the text:

Edit
Cut ✂ Ctrl X

To copy the text:

Edit
Copy 📋 Ctrl C

Position the insertion point where the selected text is to go.

Edit
Paste 📋 Ctrl V

Without the clipboard

Select the passage of text.

Press F2 to move it or ⇧ Shift F2 to copy it.

Position the insertion point and press Enter.

To move or copy the text into another document, display both document windows on the screen.

Drag the text to its new position. If you are copying, hold down the Ctrl key.

H-Inserting a hyperlink

This is a text or a graphic which you click to open another file or a Web page.

- Position the insertion point where you wish to insert the hyperlink, or select the text.

- **Insert**   🔲   Ctrl **K**
  Hyperlink

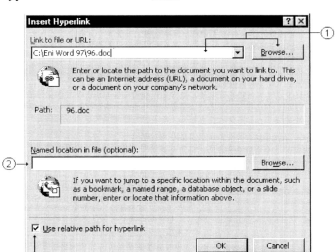

deactivate this option to use the absolute path

① Enter the name of the file to which the link refers or click the **Browse** button then select the file.

② Specify the bookmark or the range of cells... that you want to reach.

3.1 Printing options

A-Printing a document

Click the 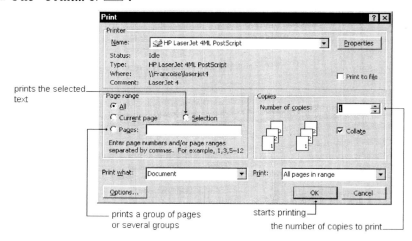 tool to print with the last options set.

B-Setting options for printing

File - Print... or Ctrl P

prints the selected text

prints a group of pages
or several groups

starts printing

the number of copies to print

C-Altering the orientation of the page

Select the text concerned, or put the insertion point towards the top of the section to be modified.

File - Page Setup...
Paper size tab

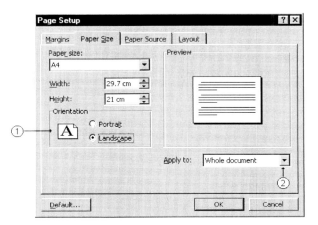

① Click the orientation you require.

② Indicate the passage concerned.

↪ *When you change the page orientation, Word takes the current values for the upper and lower margins and applies them to the left and right margins, and vice-versa.*

D-Print Preview

File
Print Preview

⌨ Ctrl F2 or Ctrl Alt

percentage of magnification

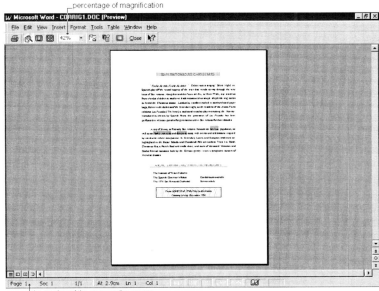

the number of the page on the screen

Microsoft Word 97

To view another page, use the scroll bar, or the keys `Pg Up` and `Pg Dn`.

To print the document, click 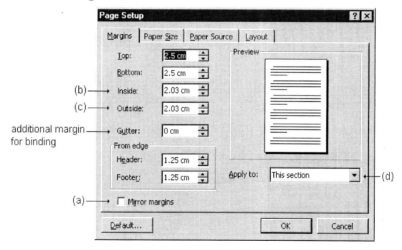; when you have finished printing, click **Close**.

To view a number of pages at once, click . Indicate how many pages you wish to see, and how they should be arranged. To return to viewing a single page, click .

To zoom in on a preview, point at the part of the text you wish to see close up and click. To return to the scaled-down presentation, click the document again.

Click for Word to repaginate the document until it gains a page.

E- Altering the margins of a document

Select the text concerned, or position the insertion point towards the top of the passage.

File - Page Setup
Select the **Margins** tab.

(a)	check the box if the document is to have different margins on odd and even pages.
(b)	the right margin of an even-numbered page, and the left one of an odd-numbered page
(c)	the left margin of an even-numbered page, and the right one of an odd-numbered page
(d)	choose the part of the document concerned.

⇨ *In **Page Layout View**, the margins can be altered by moving the corresponding markers along the horizontal and vertical rulers.*

F-Printing an envelope

If the delivery address is already entered, select it.

Tools - Envelopes and Labels

Enter the delivery address, if necessary, and the return address then click **Options...**

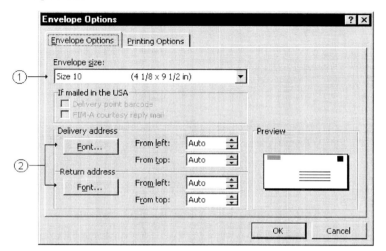

① Enter the **Envelope size**,

② Indicate how you want to present the addresses.

Under the **Printing Options** tab, choose the **Feed method** and the type of feed (**Feed from**).

Choose whether to **Print** the envelope straight away or to **Add to document**.

In the dialog box which appears, click **Yes** if you wish the address entered to become the address by default, or click **No**.

⇨ *When an envelope is added to a document, it is inserted at the top of the document as a new section. The new page created for the section is numbered 0.*

3.2 Headers and footers

A-Creating headers and footers

Position the insertion point at the beginning of the document.

View - Header and Footer

Header

Click here to switch from header to footer and back

Header and Footer

Insert AutoText ▾   Close

In the dashed box, enter the content of your header/footer, and format it as you require. You can include an existing AutoText text selected from the **Insert AutoText** list. The buttons [#], [+], [z], (clock) insert, respectively, the page number, the total number of pages, the computer's control date and the time.

Click **Close**.

⇨ *Use **File - Page Setup** to change the position of the header and footer in the top and bottom margins.*

B-Using different headers/footers in different sections

Position the insertion point in the section requiring a header/footer different from the preceding ones.

View- Header and Footer

Click the [tool] tool to deactivate it, breaking the link between the header used for previous sections and the one for the current section and those which follow it. Define the new header/footer.

C-Using different headers/footers on different pages

Position the insertion point at the beginning of the document then **View - Header and Footer**.

Click [icon]

Activate the **Layout** tab.

To use a different header/footer on the first page, activate the choice **Different first page**.
Give the header/footer for the first page.

To use different headers/footers for odd and even pages, activate the choice **Different odd and even** then click **OK**.

Enter the header/footer of the even-numbered pages, then click 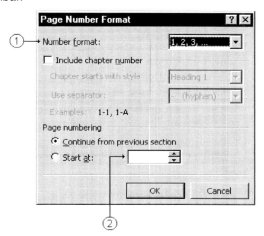 to enter the header/footer for the odd-numbered pages.

D-Changing the format of page numbers

⬛ Position the insertion point at the beginning of the section concerned.

⬛ **Insert - Page numbers**, **Format** button or click [icon] on the **Header and Footer** toolbar.

① Choose a format for the numbers.

② Give the page a new number, if you need to.

4.1 Characters

You can change the presentation of text that you have selected or set in advance the presentation of text that you are about to enter.

A-Formatting characters

Click one or more of the buttons on the Formatting bar to obtain the effect you need:

B   **Bold** type

I   *Italics*

S   <u>Underlined</u>.

Click **A ▾** or **✐ ▾** to colour the characters or to highlight them with the colour shown on the button, or open the appropriate list to choose a different colour.

Use one of the following key combinations to obtain the effect you require:

Ctrl	B	**Bold**
Ctrl	I	*Italic*
Ctrl	U	<u>Underlined</u>
Ctrl ⇧ Shift	D	<u>Double Underlined</u>
Ctrl ⇧ Shift	W	<u>Words only Underlined</u>
Ctrl ⇧ Shift	K	SMALL CAPITALS
Ctrl ⇧ Shift	A	CAPITALS
Ctrl ⇧ Shift	+	Superscript
Ctrl	=	Subscript
Ctrl ⇧ Shift	H	Hidden text

Format - Font or Ctrl **D**

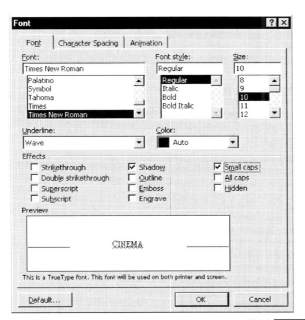

⇨ *To cancel all the formatting applied to the text, press* Ctrl space .

B-Changing the space between characters

▫ **Format - Font** or Ctrl **D**

▫ In the **Spacing** list, choose **Expanded** or **Condensed**.

▫ In the **By** box, you can enter the exact space to be left between the characters, expressed as a number of points.

C-Applying an animation effect

▫ **Format - Font** or Ctrl **D**
Animation tab

▫ Choose the effect you require.

Although you can see an animation effect on the screen, you cannot print it.

D-Changing the font and the size of characters

Select the required font and/or size from the **Font** and **Font Size** list boxes on the Formatting bar.

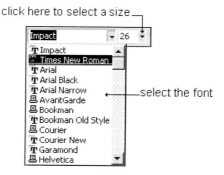

click here to select a size

select the font

E-Applying a border to characters

- Select the characters concerned.
- On the **Table and Borders** toolbar, choose a style, a line type and a colour for the border then click.

F-Changing the standard presentation of characters

- Define the new default presentation via the menu **Format - Font**.
- Click the **Default** button.
- Confirm by the **Yes** button.
- ⇨ *All characters adopt the new standard presentation, except those already formatted in a particular style.*

G-Copying formats

- Select the text whose format you wish to copy.
- Click then drag to select the text to which you want to apply the format.

4.2 Tabs

A-Setting a tab stop

You can set a tab stop which applies to paragraphs which you have selected or to the paragraphs which you are about to create.

Activate the type of tab stop required, by clicking once or several times on the button to the left of the ruler:

| **L** | left tab stop | **⊥** | centre tab stop |
| **⅃** | right tab stop | **ⅎ** | decimal tab stop. |

Click the mark on the ruler corresponding to the position you intend for the tab stop.

⇨ *When you set a personal tab stop, Word deletes any default tab stops situated in front of it.*

Format - Tabs

For each tab you wish to set:

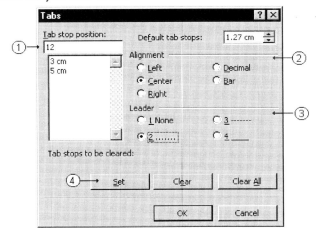

① Give the position of the tab stop.

② Choose the alignment of the tab.

③ Choose a type of leader line (or none).

④ Create the tab.

⇨ *Once a personal tab stop is displayed on the ruler, just double-click it to activate the **Tabs** dialog box from the **Format** menu.*

B-Managing existing tab stops

To move a tab stop, drag its marker to a new position.

To delete a tab stop, drag its marker right off the ruler. To delete all the tabs, go into the **Tabs** dialog box, and click the **Clear All** button.

4.3 Formatting paragraphs

*The formatting that you define applies to the current paragraph or to the paragraphs you select. To open the **Paragraph** dialog box, use the command **Format - Paragraph** or double-click the indentation marker.*

A-Indentation of paragraphs

Drag the indentation markers on the ruler to the required position.

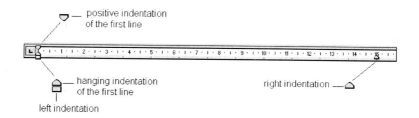

positive indentation
of the first line

hanging indentation
of the first line

right indentation

left indentation

⇨ *You can also use the* *and* ⊞ *buttons to move the left indentation to the next tab stop, or the preceding one.*

Format - Paragraph...
Indents and Spacing tab

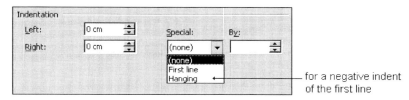

for a negative indent
of the first line

⇨ *It is possible to set a negative indentation beyond the edge of the page (0 on the ruler), so that text can be entered in the left margin.*

B-Modifying the alignment of paragraphs

Alignment	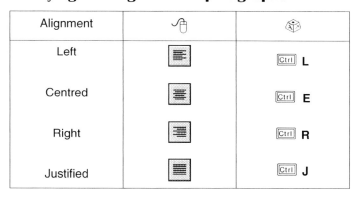	
Left	🖱	Ctrl L
Centred	🖱	Ctrl E
Right	🖱	Ctrl R
Justified	🖱	Ctrl J

⇨ *These alignments are also accessible by **Format - Paragraph**.*

C-Modifying the line spacing

Format - Paragraph...
Indents and Spacing tab

Choose a value from the **Line spacing** list box:

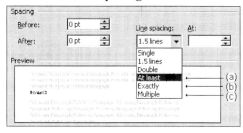

(a)   minimum value of line spacing (enter the value in the **At:** box).

(b)   the value remains fixed: Word cannot alter it whatever the size of the characters (enter the value in the **At:** box).

(c)   each line is spaced according to its tallest character.

D-Modifying the spacing of paragraphs

▓ **Format - Paragraph**
Indents and Spacing tab

▓ Under **Spacing**, define the value of space to be left **Before** and/or **After** a paragraph.

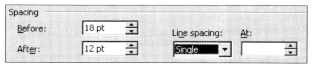

⇨ *On the keyboard, press* [Ctrl] *0 to leave a blank line (12 pt) above each selected paragraph (and again to remove it).*

E-Preventing a break within/between paragraphs

▓ To prevent a page/column break within a paragraph, select that paragraph; to avoid a break between two paragraphs, select the first; to keep several paragraphs together, select all except the last.

▓ **Format - Paragraph**
Line and Page Breaks tab

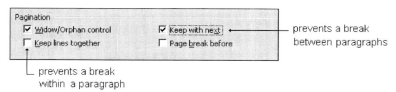

F-Applying the default presentation to paragraphs

▓ To return the current paragraph (or the selected paragraphs) to the default presentation, press [Ctrl] **Q**.

⇨ *To change the default format used for paragraphs, modify the style called **Normal**.*

4.4 Paragraph borders

Display or hide the Borders toolbar by clicking 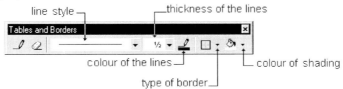.

A-Applying a border

- Select the paragraphs concerned.
- Choose the style, thickness and colour of the lines then click the button corrresponding to the type of border you require.

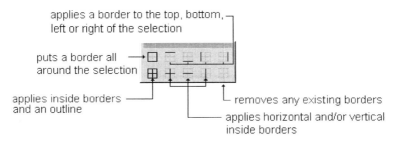

↪ *The border extends from the left indent to the right indent.*

↪ *If you type three dashes (---) or three equal signs (===) at the beginning of a new paragraph, Word applies a one- or two-line border to the paragraph.*

↪ *Borders are also accessible via **Format - Borders and Shading**.*

B-Modifying the space left between the text and the lines

- Select the paragraphs concerned.
- **Format - Borders and Shading**
  Borders tab.
- Click the **Options** button then give the spaces between the text and the border in the **From text** box.

C-Shading a paragraph

Select the paragraphs concerned.

Choose the shading from the [icon] list on the Borders toolbar.

Format - Borders and Shading
Shading tab

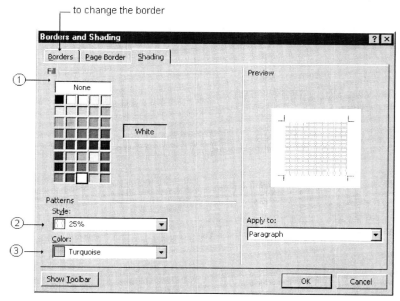

— to change the border

① Choose the background.

② Choose a pattern.

③ Choose a colour for the pattern.

4.5 Presentation techniques

A-Applying a border to a page

Format - Borders and shading
Page Border tab

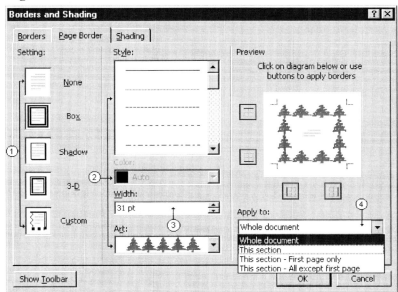

① Choose the type of border you require:

② Choose the style and colour of the border, or if you prefer, choose a pattern.

③ Give the width of the border.

④ Choose the part of the document to which you wish to apply the border.

B-Applying a background

A background applies to an entire document. Although you can see the background on the screen, you cannot print it.

Format - Background

Choose a colour for the background or click **Fill Effects**.

Click the tab that interests you, and set the options.

FORMATTING

C-Creating a Drop Cap

Select the future drop cap then use **Format - Drop Cap....**

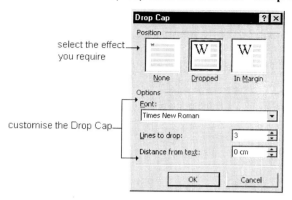

select the effect you require

customise the Drop Cap

D-Inserting a WordArt text effect

Use WordArt to introduce special typographic effects into your text.

Click the 🔳 button on the Drawing toolbar.

Choose the effect you wish to apply then enter.

Type in your text, using ⟦Enter⟧ to change line.

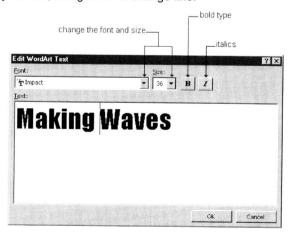

bold type

change the font and size

italics

Click **OK**.

E- Editing WordArt text

Click the WordArt object to select it and use the buttons on the WordArt toolbar to edit it.

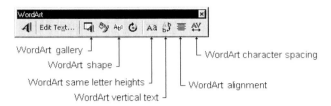

WordArt gallery
WordArt shape
WordArt same letter heights
WordArt vertical text
WordArt character spacing
WordArt alignment

F- Numbering and Bullets

Select the paragraphs you wish to format, if they are already entered then click:

to number the selected paragraphs.

to put a bullet before each paragraph.

Format - Bullets and Numbering

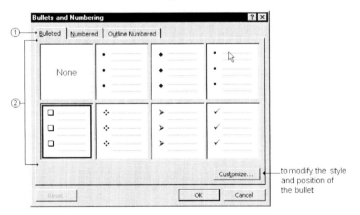

to modify the style and position of the bullet

① Choose the type of list.
② Click the model you prefer.

FORMATTING

G-Presenting text in columns

Format - Columns

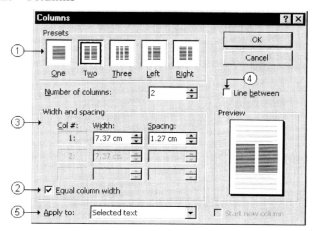

① Choose the basic presentation you require.

② Indicate whether or not all the columns are to be of identical width.

③ If necessary, change the width and spacing for each column.

④ Check the box to separate the columns with a line.

⑤ Indicate the part of the text to be presented in columns.

⇨ *The* ▦ *tool can also be used to put text into columns.*

⇨ *To view the presentation in columns, you must be in Page Layout view.*

⇨ *To insert a column break, press* [Ctrl] [⇧ Shift] [Enter] *.*

H-Inserting a picture/a sound/a video

■ **Insert - Picture - Clip Art**

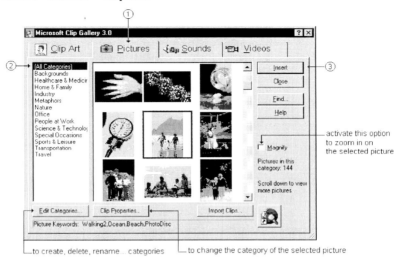

① Activate the appropriate tab.

② Select a category then an object.

③ Insert the object.

⇨ *To resize the picture without distorting it, drag the handle at one of its corners, or use Format - Picture.*

⇨ *To crop the picture, click* ![icon] *and drag one of the handles.*

⇨ *To play a sound or a video, double-click it.*

I- Wrapping a picture/drawing/text box

■ Select the object concerned.

■ **Format - AutoShape** or **Picture**
Wrapping tab

Microsoft Word 97

41

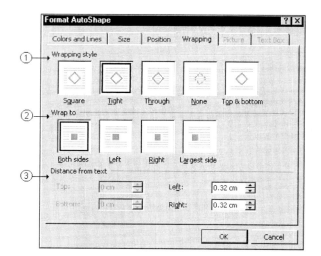

① Indicate how the text should be arranged around the object.
② Indicate where (on which sides of the object) to position the text.
③ Give the distance between the text and the edge of the object.

J- Attaching a caption to an object

Select the object concerned then use **Insert - Caption**.

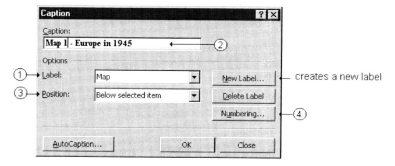

creates a new label

① Choose the part of the caption which will be common to all objects of the same type.
② Fill in the rest of the caption.
③ Indicate its position.
④ Choose the format for caption numbers.
Click **OK** once more to insert the caption.

5.1 Drawing objects

A-Drawing a simple shape

- Display the **Drawing** toolbar.
- Click the one of the tool buttons: [▧], [▧], [▢], [◯] then drag to draw the shape.

⇨ *To obtain a perfect square or circle, hold down the* ⌷Shift⌷ *key while drawing with the rectangle/ellipse tool. To draw a rectangle/square or an ellipse/circle beginning in the centre rather than from an edge, hold the* ⌷Ctrl⌷ *key down while you are drawing.*

B-Drawing an AutoShape

- Open the **AutoShapes** list on the Drawing toolbar then choose a category and a shape. Drag to draw the shape.

C-Selecting objects

- If necessary, click [▨].
- <u>For one object</u>: click the object.
- <u>For several objects</u>: select the first, then hold down ⌷Shift⌷ as you select the others. Alternatively, drag to surround all the objects.
- To cancel a selection, click an empty space.

D-Sizing/moving an object

- To size an object, select it then drag one of the selection handles.
- To move an object, select it and point the selection. When the pointer takes the form of four arrows, drag the shape to move it.

E-Creating a text box

Creating a text box allows you to position text anywhere on the page.

- Click [▨] then drag to draw the text box.
- Type your text as you would type an ordinary paragraph.
- Click outside the box when you have finished.

⇨ *Use the usual commands to format the text.*

⇨ *If the text box is too small to display all the text you enter, only part of the text will be visible.*

DRAWING

⇨ *To establish a link with a second text box which will take the overflow, select the first text box, open the shortcut menu and choose* **Create Text Box Link** *then click the second text box.*

F-Aligning objects relative to one another

▨ Open the **Draw** list on the Drawing toolbar and activate **Align or Distribute**.

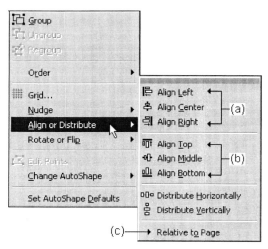

(a) vertical alignment.

(b) horizontal alignment.

(c) activate this object to align objects relative not to one another but to the page.

G-Rotating or flipping an object

Free rotation

▨ Select the object then click ⟳.

▨ Drag one of the object's selection handles, and pivot the object to achieve the result you require.

When you have finished, click ⟳ again.

Flipping an object, or rotation through 90°

▨ Select the object.

▨ Open the **Draw** list on the Drawing toolbar and choose **Rotate or Flip**.

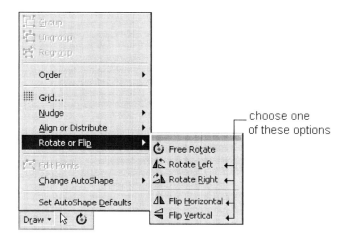

choose one
of these options

H-Grouping/ungrouping objects

You can group several objects (so that they can be moved all at once, for example), or separate an existing group.

▪ Select the objects.

▪ Open the **Draw** list on the **Drawing** toolbar.

▪ Choose **Group** or **Ungroup**.

I- Reorganising overlapping objects

▪ Select the object.

▪ Open the **Draw** list on the **Drawing** toolbar.

▪ Choose **Order**.

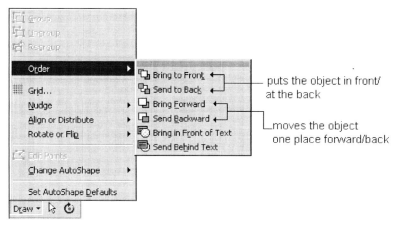

puts the object in front/
at the back

moves the object
one place forward/back

DRAWING

Microsoft Word 97

J- Activating and deactivating snap to grid

Open the **Draw** list on the Drawing toolbar then choose **Grid**....

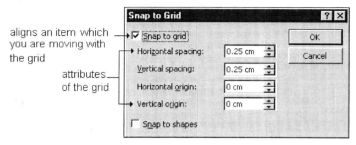

aligns an item which
you are moving with
the grid

attributes
of the grid

5.2 Formatting objects

A- Colouring an object or applying a texture

Select the object concerned.

Open the 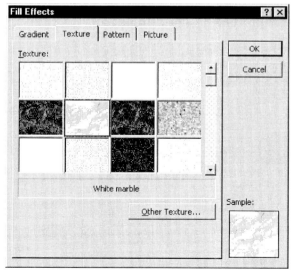 list and choose a colour. To apply shading, textures and patterns to the object or even to insert a picture, click **Fill Effects**:

B-Modifying the outline of an object

▨ Select the object.

▨ Click ▤ to change the style and thickness of the line.

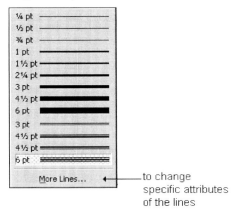

to change
specific attributes
of the lines

▨ Click ▥ for dots and dashes.

▨ Click ▨ to change the colour of the outline.

C-Rounding the corners of a rectangle

▨ Select the rectangle concerned.
▨ Open the **Draw** list on the **Drawing** toolbar.
▨ Activate the **Change AutoShape** option. In the **Basic Shapes** list, choose the rectangle with rounded corners.

D-Giving a shadow to an object

▨ Select the object and click ▣.
▨ Choose the shadow effect you require.

E-Applying a 3D effect

Select the object then click 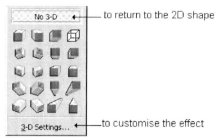.

to return to the 2D shape

to customise the effect

F-Adding text to a shape

Select the shape.

Right-click it to open the shortcut menu and choose **Add Text**.

Enter the text then click outside the shape.

6.1 Templates

A- Creating a document template

A document template allows you to save and reuse styles of presentation and/or text.

▦ **File - New...**

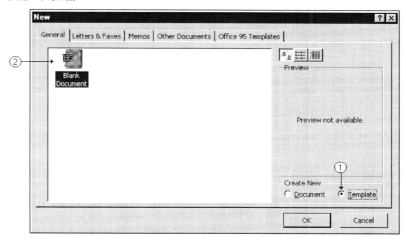

① Click the **Template** option.

② To base your new template on another, select the existing template.

▦ Save the template in the same way as you would save an ordinary document. Templates are usually saved in the **Templates** folder, situated in the folder where Word or Microsoft Office is installed.

⇨ *The extension attributed to a template is .DOT.*

B- Creating a document based on a template

Documents based on a particular template have access to the styles (or the text) saved in it.

▦ **File - New...**

TEMPLATES/STYLES/AUTOTEXTS

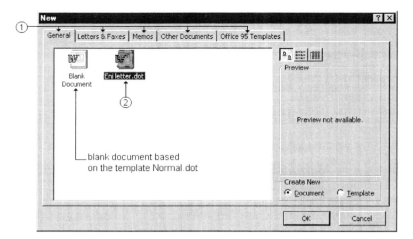

① Choose a category of template.

② Double-click the name of the template.

C-Opening a document template

You will need to open the template if you want to make changes in it.

■ **File**   Ctrl O
Open...

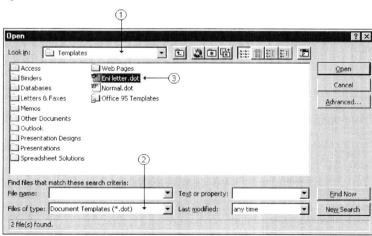

① Open the **Templates** folder.

② Select **Document Templates**.

③ Double-click the name of the template you wish to open.

⇨ *When you want to save the changes you have made, check that **Document Templates** appears in the **Files of type** box.*

D-Linking another template to an existing document

This technique enables you to use the styles of a template other than the one you have used to create the active document.

- **Tools - Templates and Add-Ins**
- Click the **Attach...** button.
- Double-click the name of the template.
- Activate the choice **Automatically update document styles**.

6.2 Styles

A-Creating a style

In a style, several elements of formatting are saved together so that they can be applied simultaneously.

Based on existing formatting

- Select the contents of the **Style** list box on the Formatting toolbar.
- Type a name for the new style and press ⌷Enter⌷ .
- ⇨ *The style is immediately applied to the current paragraph.*

With no example of formatting

- **Format - Style**
- Click the **New** button.

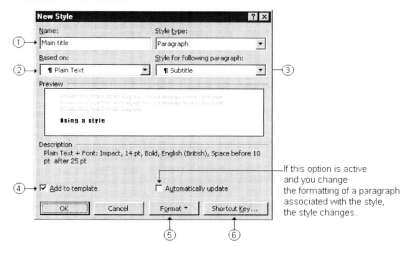

If this option is active and you change the formatting of a paragraph associated with the style, the style changes.

① Give a name for the style.

TEMPLATES/STYLES/AUTOTEXTS

② Select a basic style which you can modify to create the new style.

③ Select the style which should be applied to the paragraph which follows.

④ Activate this option to add the style to the template associated with the current document.

⑤ Click this button to define the formatting included in the style.

⑥ If you wish, assign a shortcut key to the style.

⇨ *If you are going to use the style in more than one document, you should create it in a template.*

B-Applying a style

▒ If necessary, select the text concerned.

▒ Open the **Styles** list on the Formatting toolbar and select the style, or press the shortcut key.

⇨ *To return the text to the style* Normal, *press* Ctrl ⇧ Shift *N*.

C-Modifying/deleting a style

▒ **Format - Style**

▒ Select the style.

▒ Click the **Modify** button and change the details of the style.

*The option **Add to template** makes the same changes in the template linked to the current document.*

▒ To delete a style, click the **Delete** button and click **Yes** to confirm.

D-Printing the list of styles

- File - Print... or ⌨Ctrl P
- Open the **Print what** list and choose **Styles**.

E-Using styles from another template

- Apply the existing styles to your document.
- **Format - Style Gallery**

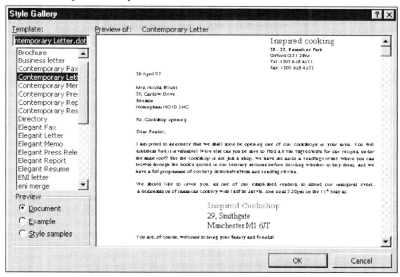

- Choose a **Template** in the list, and check the result under **Preview of**.

F-Using autoformat for your document

- Open the document.
- **Format - AutoFormat...**
- If necessary, click the **Options...** button.

TEMPLATES/STYLES/AUTOTEXTS

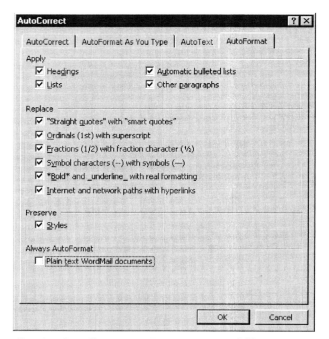

- Personalise the **AutoFormat** options, then click **OK**.
- Choose **AutoFormat now** or **AutoFormat and review each change**, then click **OK.**
- You can choose to **Accept All** the new format, to **Reject All** and leave your document unchanged, or to **Review Changes** and check each modification one at a time.
- If you choose this last option, Word stops at each of the revision marks placed in the text, and prompts you to accept or reject the change.

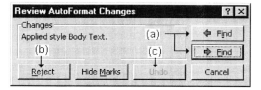

(a)   to go to the next mark or the one before.

(b)   to refuse the modification.

(c)   to reinstate a correction just cancelled.

6.3 AutoTexts

Creating an AutoText to represent a text which you often have to type (address, form of words ...) allows you to use an abbreviation to insert it.

A-Creating an AutoText entry

- If you are going to use the AutoText in documents based on a particular template, open one of the documents then click 🖳 on the AutoText toolbar. Select the template from the **Look in** list then click **OK**.

- Activate the style to which the AutoText will be linked then enter the contents of the AutoText, not forgetting layout and blank lines. Select the contents of the AutoText.

- **Insert - AutoText - AutoText** or click 🖳.

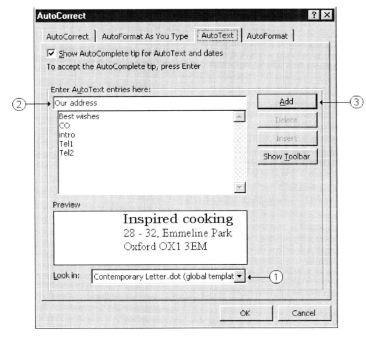

① Choose the template in which you want to create the AutoText.

② Give an abbreviation for the text you have selected.

③ Create the AutoText.

↪ *Once you have specified a template for the AutoTexts in the **AutoCorrect** dialog box, you can use the **New** button on the **AutoText** toolbar to create new entries.*

TEMPLATES/STYLES/AUTOTEXTS

⮑ *If you have created the AutoTexts in a template other than NOR-MAL.DOT, Word prompts you to save them when you close or save the document. If you have created them in NORMAL.DOT, Word prompts you to save them as you leave the program.*

B-Using an AutoText

⬡ Enter the abbreviation then press ⌨F3⌨.

🖱 **Insert - AutoText** or open the **All Entries** list on the **AutoText** toolbar.

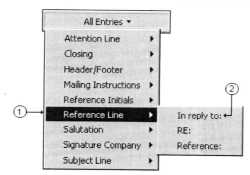

① Choose the style linked to the AutoText.
② Select the AutoText.

C-Managing existing AutoTexts

🖱 **Insert - AutoText - AutoText** or click .

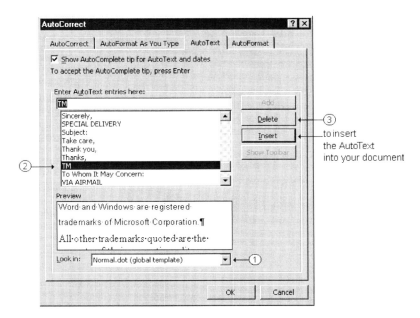

① Indicate the name of the template containing the AutoText.

② Click the name of the AutoText you wish to delete.

③ Delete it.

░ If you want to make changes to the content of an AutoText, you must create a new one with the same name.

░ To print the list of AutoTexts, use **File** - **Print**. In the **Print what** list, choose **AutoText entries**.

TEMPLATES/STYLES/AUTOTEXTS

7.1 Finding/replacing text

A-Finding text

By its content

■ Position the insertion point where you want to start searching.
■ **Edit - Find** or Ctrl **F**
■ To make the search criteria more precise, click the **More** button.

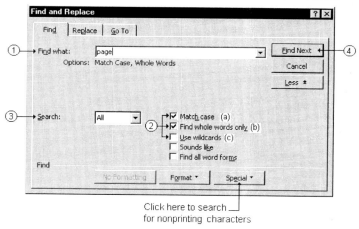

Click here to search
for nonprinting characters

① Enter the text you want to find.

② Give details of how you want to search:

(a)   to find the text in question, written with the exact combination of upper and lower case letters entered in the **Find what** box.

(b)   if the character string you are looking for constitutes a word.

(c)   to use wildcard characters to represent part of the text you are searching for, for example:

?   represents a single character (?aw: saw, law, raw...).

*   represents a string of any length (s*w: saw, somehow...).

[ab]   represents any one of the characters between the brackets (drive[nrs]: driven, driver, drives).

[!]   represents any character except the one inside the brackets (th[!i]n: than, then, not thin).

<   represents the beginning of a word (<in): ink, investigate, not drive-in).

>   represents the end of a word ((re>): centre, not rewrite).

③ Indicate the direction for the search.

④ Start the search.

Almost immediately, the first occurrence of the text in the document is selected.

If this first text is the one you are looking for, close the dialog box using **Cancel**; if it is not, continue by **Find Next**.

⇨ *Once the **Find** dialog box is closed, you can go on searching using* 0 Shift F4 *.*

By its format

In the **Find** dialog box, click the **Format** button and indicate the category of formatting which interests you.

In the dialog box, activate the attributes applied to the text you want to find and make sure that no others are activated.

If you need to, give details of other categories of formatting, then start the search by clicking **Find Next**.

B-Replacing one text by another

Position the insertion point where you want Word to start looking for the text.

Edit - Replace or Ctrl **H**

To make the search criteria more precise, click the **More** button.

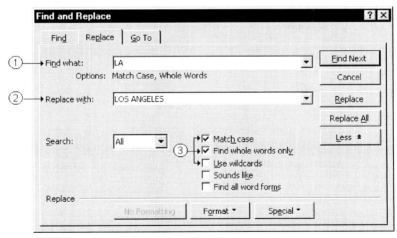

① Enter the text you are looking for.

② Enter the new text.

③ Set the search criteria.

To make the replacements one at a time, click **Find Next** then **Replace**; to replace all occurrences of the text at once, click **Replace All**.

⇨ *Use the same command to replace one format by another.*

7.2 Spelling/Grammar/Thesaurus

A-Checking the grammar or spelling in a document

Setting off a spelling check

To check the whole document, position the insertion point at the top. If only a part of the text is concerned, select it.

Tools F7
Spelling and Grammar

Managing correctly spelt words

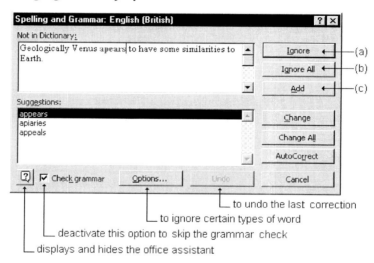

(a) leaves the word as it is and continues the spelling check.

(b) ignores the word each time it occurs during the check.

(c) adds the word to a custom dictionary so that Word will recognise it the next time.

Correcting badly spelt words

If the correct version of the word is proposed in the **Suggestions** list, double-click the right spelling. If you know the correct spelling, enter it in the text box and click **Change**, or click **Change All** to correct the same error each time it recurs in the document.

To correct an unwanted repetition, click the **Delete** button.

⇨ *Spelling is checked against Word's main dictionary and as many personal dictionaries as you like (by default, there exists only one: CUSTOM.DIC).*

Managing errors in grammar

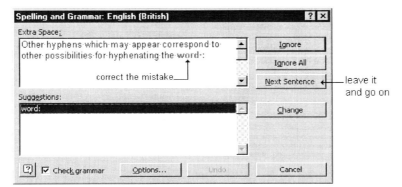

Using a custom dictionary

Click the **Options...** button in the **Spelling and Grammar** dialog box then the **Dictionaries** button.

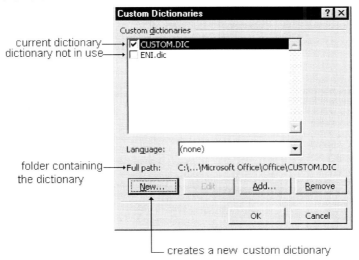

Choose the dictionary that you want to use from the **Custom Dictionaries** list in the **Spelling and Grammar** dialog box.

↪ *To consult a personal dictionary, open the corresponding document (with extension .DIC).*

B-Activating AutoCorrect

Word corrects common mistakes as you type.

Tools - AutoCorrect

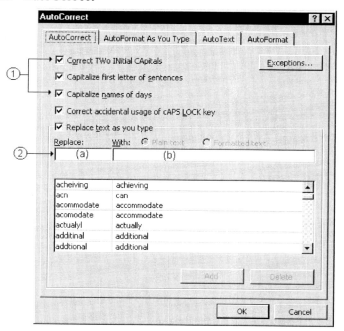

① Activate or deactivate the first three options.

② If you often make the same mistake, type the incorrect version of the word in (a), and the correct version in (b) then click **Add**.

C-Using the thesaurus

Place the insertion point in the word, or just after it.

Tools - Language - Thesaurus... or ⇧ Shift F7

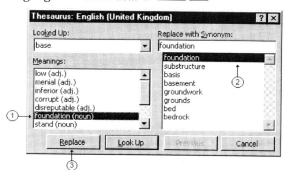

① Select the correct meaning for the word.

② Select a synonym.

③ Replace the word by its synonym.

⇨ *To list synonyms of one of the synonyms, double-click it (click **Previous** to return to a word looked up earlier).*

7.3 Revising text

A-Hyphenating Words

If you want to carry out hyphenation of the whole document, place the insertion point at the beginning, if not, select the passage concerned.

Tools - Language - Hyphenation

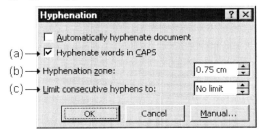

(a)   If this choice is deactivated, Word will not hyphenate words with capital letters.

(b)   If the space available on a line is superior to the value of the hyphenation zone, Word tries to break up the first word of the following line.

(c)   The usual value is three.

If you want Word to do all the hyphenating without prompting you for confirmation, activate **Automatically hyphenate document** then click **OK**.

To confirm each separate case, click **Manual**:

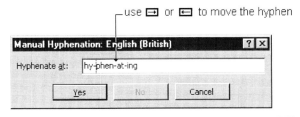

⇨ *You can insert an optional hyphen into the text by pressing* Ctrl -.

B-Keeping track of revisions

▒ Open the document.

▒ **Tools - Track Changes - Highlight Changes**

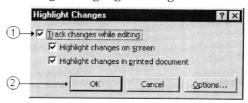

① Activate this option.

② Go into tracking mode.

▒ Insert, delete or move text or add comments.

Word highlights the changes you make.

Inserting a comment

▒ Position the insertion point.

▒ **Insert - Comment**

▒ Enter the text then click **Close**.

A comment appears as a pale yellow ScreenTip.

Accepting/rejecting changes

▒ **Tools - Track Changes - Accept or Reject Changes**.

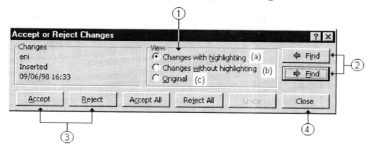

① Indicate how you want to view the document:

   (a)   the revisions to the text appear underlined and in colour.

   (b)   shows the document as it will look if you accept all the revisions.

   (c)   shows the original document (without revisions).

② Click these buttons to move from revision to revision.

③ Accept or refuse the modification.

④ Close the dialog box.

▒ Come out of tracking mode by double-clicking the TRK indicator on the status bar.

8.1 Notes and bookmarks

A-Creating notes

This section deals with footnotes and endnotes.

Position the insertion point at the place in the document where you want to insert a note reference.

Insert - Footnote

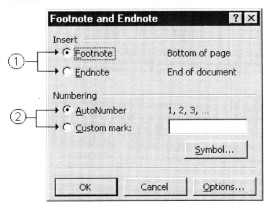

① Specify whether you are creating a footnote or an endnote.

② Decide how you want the note references to appear.

Enter the text of the note in the note pane (visible in **Normal** view).

Click in the workspace or press F6 .

To see the text of a note, point to the note reference (the content of the note appears in a ScreenTip, providing the **ScreenTips** option is active in the **Tools - Options** dialog box) or use the note pane.

B-Closing/opening the pane

View - Footnotes or Alt X

When the pane is open, you can shut it by clicking the **Close** button or pressing Alt ⇧ Shift F. When it is closed, it can be opened by a double-click on a note reference.

C-Managing existing notes

To delete a note, select its note reference then press the Del key.

To move a note, move the note reference as you would a text.

To modify the text of a note, double-click the note reference.

⮡ *The notes are automatically renumbered afterwards.*

D-Changing the look of the notes

▨ **Insert - Footnote**

▨ Click the **Options...** button.

▨ In the **Place at** list box, indicate the note's position on the printed page.

▨ Modify the numbering:

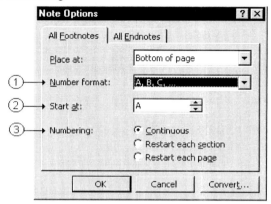

① Select a format for the numbers.

② Change the first number, if necessary.

③ Choose one of the continuity options.

▨ To change the way the notes look, modify the styles associated with them: **Footnote Reference**, **Endnote Reference**, **Footnote Text**, **Endnote Text**.

E-Working with bookmarks

A bookmark allows you to mark a place in a text so that you can find it more quickly.

Creating a bookmark

▨ If going to a bookmark involves selecting a passage of text, select that text. If going to a bookmark is simply a matter of moving the insertion point, put the insertion point in the position required.

▨ **Insert Bookmark...** or Ctrl 0 Shift F5

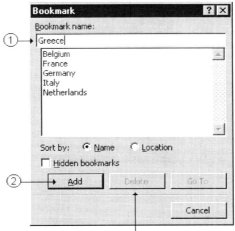

deletes the selected bookmark

① Enter the name of the new bookmark (20 characters maximum).

② Create the bookmark.

Using a bookmark

▦ **Insert - Bookmark...** or `Ctrl` `⇧ Shift` `F 5`

▦ In **Sort by**, choose to sort the bookmark list by the **Location** of the bookmark in the document, or by its **Name**.

▦ Double-click the bookmark you wish to find then shut the dialog box using the **Close** button.

⇨ *You can also reach a bookmark via **Edit - Go To**.*

8.2 Outlines/Table of contents/Index

A-Creating master documents

A master document groups together several sub-documents for the purposes of numbering their pages, adding headings, notes...

▦ Create a new document using the template common to all the sub-documents.

▦ **View - Master Document**

▦ Insert each sub-document by clicking ⬓.

▦ Save this new master document.

▦ If necessary, number the pages, headings... from within the master document.

▦ To print all the sub-documents, print the master document.

B-Creating a summary of a document

Open the document concerned.

Tools - AutoSummarize...

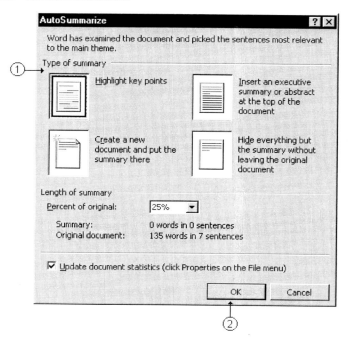

① Choose the type of summary you require.
② Create the summary.

C-Planning the outline of a document

Making an outline not only allows you to put together a table of contents, but also facilitates moving around in the document. There are two ways of making an outline: using Outline view or assigning importance levels.

D-Using Outline view

Activating/leaving Outline view

View
Outline

Leave outline view by **View - Normal** or **View - Page Layout**.

Entering a heading into the outline

▨ Apply one of the following styles, depending on the importance of the heading:

Heading 1   main headings
Heading 2   subheadings
Heading 3   sub-subheadings

or use the ⬅ and ➡ buttons.

⇨ *Applying the styles Heading 1, Heading 2, Heading 3... obviously cancels any existing formatting of your own. You can however, customise these styles once they are in place.*

⇨ *A cross to the left of the text marks it out as being a heading in an outline.*

E-Assigning an importance level to a paragraph

This technique allows you to create an outline without loosing the existing formatting.

▨ Select the paragraph which corresponds to the heading.

▨ **Format - Paragraph**
Indents and spacing tab

▨ In the **Outline level** list, choose the level for the heading.

▨ Enter.

⇨ *Repeat for each level of heading.*

⇨ *If you plan to number the headings in an outline created using this technique, put the corresponding paragraphs into a style which includes numbering.*

⇨ *You can also include an outline level in a style.*

F- Using the outline of a document

 In Outline view, use the buttons on the toolbar:

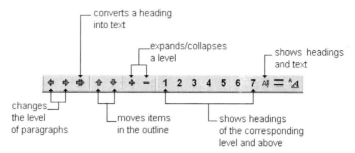

converts a heading
into text

expands/collapses
a level

shows headings
and text

changes
the level
of paragraphs

moves items
in the outline

shows headings
of the corresponding
level and above

| Alt | ⇧ Shift | n° | displays headings of the specified level and above. |

- or + (on number pad) : hides or shows the text under the heading.

⇨ *An outline can be printed.*

⇨ *You can change the order of headings in an outline by dragging a heading to a new position.*

G-Numbering headings

Format - Bullets and Numbering...
Outline Numbered tab

To number outline headings created by applying the styles **Heading 1, Heading 2**..., choose one of the options where the word **Heading** appears.

To number the headings in an outline created by applying importance levels to paragraphs (these paragraphs must be in a style which includes numbering), choose one of the options then click **Customize** and, if necessary, **More**.

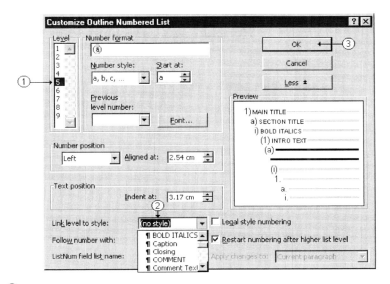

① Select the level.

② Choose the style of the paragraphs.

③ Enter when you have defined every level.

H-Constructing a table of contents from an outline

▓ Place the insertion point where the table is to be inserted.

▓ **Insert - Index and Tables...**
Table of Contents tab

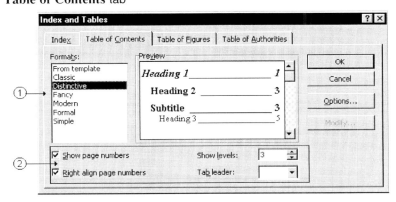

① Choose the format you prefer.

② Set the formatting options.

↪ *A table created by this method uses the styles TOC1 and TOC2, which you can, of course, customise.*

I- Inserting a table of figures

Place the insertion point where the table of figures is to be inserted.

Insert - Index and Tables...
Table of figures tab

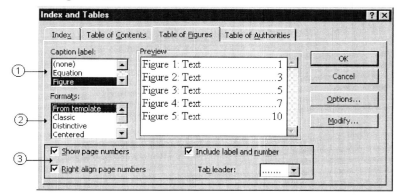

① Indicate the type of item listed in the table (figures, equations, photos...).

② Choose the style you prefer.

③ Set the formatting options.

J- Making an index

Defining an entry for the index

If the entry you want in the index is already entered, select it, otherwise place the insertion point where the subject to be indexed is discussed.

Insert - Index and Tables...   [Alt] [⇧ Shift] **X**
Index tab
Mark Entry button

If appropriate, specify the **Main entry** in the box provided.

If necessary, go to the **Subentry** box and type in the secondary entry.

If you wish to create further entry levels, type a colon (:) before entering the text.

Format the text using shortcut keys.

Enter by clicking the **Mark** button then click **Close**.

⇨ *If the nonprinting characters are visible, you will be able to see the inserted field {XE. ...}.*

Inserting the index

░ Place the insertion point where you want to put the index.

░ **Insert - Index and Tables...**
Index tab

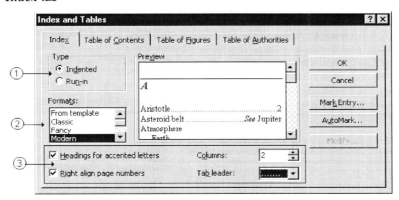

① Choose a look for the subentries.

② Select a format.

③ Set the formatting options.

▷ *The styles used in the table are called **Index 1**, **Index 2**... They can, of course, be modified.*

9.1 Creating a table

A-Inserting a table

Display the **Tables and borders** toolbar by clicking the button .

Activate the tool, if necessary. The mouse pointer takes the shape of a pencil.

Choose a style, thickness and colour for the outline of the table.

Drag to draw the outline, then draw in the lines between the rows and columns.

Click to deactivate the tool.

Position the insertion point where you want to insert the table.

Table - Insert Table...

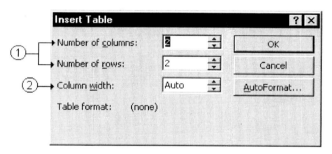

① Specify the number of columns and the number of rows.

② Let Word decide the width of each column (**Auto**), or enter your own value.

↪ *A table can contain a maximum of 63 columns.*

↪ *You can also insert a table using the button.*

B-Moving around a table

Use the following keys:

⇄ / ⇧ Shift ⇄	cell to the right/left.
↓ / ↑	cell below/above.
Alt Home / Alt End	first/last cell of the active row.
Alt Pg Up / Alt Pg Dn	first/last cell of the active column.

C-Filling in a table

░ Click inside a cell and enter its contents in the same way as you enter any other text.

░ Tabs can be set in a table: to go to any tab stop other than a decimal one, press Ctrl ⇄ .

D-Selecting in a table

░ Depending on what you are selecting, use one of the following techniques:

	🖰	📄	🎲
Cell	Point to the edge of the cell and click		⇄ or ⇧ Shift ⇄
Column	point to the line at the top of the column and click	**Table - Select Column**	Ctrl Alt L
Row	point just to the left of the first cell and click	**Table - Select Row**	
Table	drag or use ⇧ Shift + click	**Table - Select Table**	Alt 5 (with number lock off)

⮕ *To cancel the selection, click outside it.*

E-Inserting a column/row

░ Select the column or the row just after the position where you are going to insert the new one. To insert a new column at the end of the table, select the symbols to the right of the last column.

░ **Table - Insert Columns**

or

Table - Insert Rows

⮕ *To add a row at the bottom of the table, click in the last cell and press* ⇄ .

F- Inserting cells into a table

░ Select the cells which come after the position where you are going to insert the new ones.

░ Table - Insert Cells...

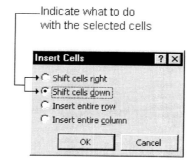

Indicate what to do with the selected cells

G-Deleting rows/columns/cells

Rows and/or columns

░ Select the rows/columns you want deleted.

░ Table
Delete Rows or Delete Columns

Cells

░ Select the cells to be deleted.

░ Table - Delete Cells...

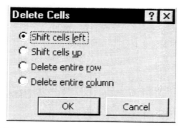

░ Decide what should happen to the remaining cells.

H-Splitting a table in two

░ Place the insertion point in the row below the point where you are going to split the table.

░ Table - Split Table

I- Merging cells

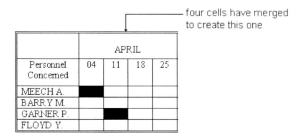

four cells have merged to create this one

Click the [image] tool button.

Erase the line which separates the cells you wish to merge.

Click [image] to deactivate it.

Select the cells you wish to merge.

Table
Merge Cells

J- Splitting cells

Select the cell(s) you wish to split

Table
Split Cells

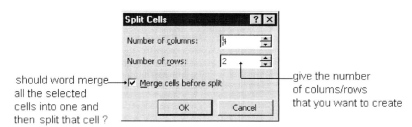

should word merge all the selected cells into one and then split that cell ?

give the number of colums/rows that you want to create

K-Sorting a table

▨ Table - Sort... For each criterion:

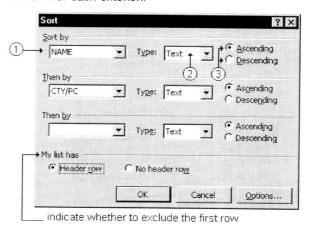

① Select the number of the column.

② Indicate what type of data the column contains.

③ Choose the sort order.

⇨ *You can also sort the table using the* ⊞ *and* ⊞ *buttons.*

L-Converting text into a table

▨ Select the text then use **Table - Convert Text To Table...**

▨ Confirm by **OK**.

9.2 Formatting a table

A-Modifying column width/row height

For a row, drag the line underneath the row until you are satisfied with the new width.

For a column, drag the line at the right of the column or the marker on the ruler.

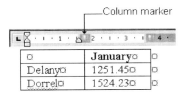
Column marker

Depending on how you drag, you obtain different effects:

mouse alone — to modify the width of the particular column and compensate by changing the width of the column on the right.

with ⇧ Shift — to modify the width of the particular column without adjusting any others. The overall width of the table is affected.

with Ctrl ⇧ Shift — to modify the width of the particular column, and adjust all columns to the right, to preserve the overall width of the table.

↪ *If you hold down the* Alt *key as you drag, the dimensions of the co-lumn/row appear on the ruler.*

Select the columns, or rows: they will all be given the same new width/height.

Table - Cell Height and Width...

Changing the width of columns

Column tab

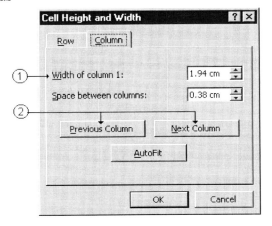

① Enter the new width of the column.

② If the next column (or the previous column) also needs modifying click the appropriate button.

Microsoft Word 97

Changing the height of rows

▓ **Row** tab

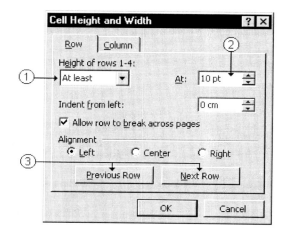

① Choose:

Auto	to let Word decide the height.
At least	to define a minimum height.
Exactly	to define a fixed height.

② Unless you have chosen **Auto**, enter the new height.

③ If the next row (or the one before) also needs modifying click the appropriate button.

▷ *To standardise the height (or width) of several rows (or columns), select them then click* ⊞ *or* ⊞ .

B-Modifying the vertical alignment of cell contents

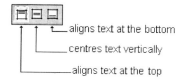

aligns text at the bottom

centres text vertically

aligns text at the top

▷ *To change the orientation of text in a cell, use the* ⊞ *button.*

C-Formatting a table automatically

Click in the table you wish to format then use **Table - Table AutoFormat...** or ![icon].

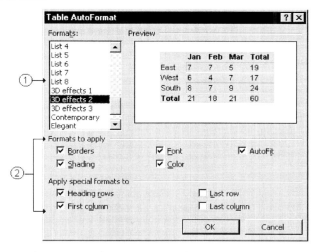

① Choose the presentation closest to what you have in mind.

② Choose the **Formats to apply**, and indicate what they should apply to.

⇨ *To format the content of a cell, use the techniques you use to format paragraphs.*

⇨ *Use the tools from the **Tables and Borders** toolbar to apply borders to the cells.*

D-Fixing column headings

If the table takes up several pages, this technique allows the column headings to be printed at the top of each page.

Select the rows containing the headings.

Table - Headings

E-Positioning a table on the page

Select the entire table then use **Table - Cell Height and Width, Row** tab.

In the **Alignment** group, choose the position you want for the table.

TABLES/CHARTS

9.3 Calculations/Charts

A-Adding up a column/row

Click the cell where you want to display the result then click $\boxed{\Sigma}$ in the **Table and Borders** toolbar.

⇨ *Word adds the contents of the cells above the result cell.*

B-Managing a table as with a spreadsheet

Each column is identified by a letter (the first column is A, the second column is B ...) and each row by a number (the first row is 1, the second row is 2 ...). The cell reference is the association of its column letter with its row number (A2, B5...).

To refer to consecutive cells, give the reference of the first cell, type a colon (:), and the reference of the last cell (eg. C2: C4). To refer to non-consecutive cells, use the comma as the separator (eg. B5, D5).

Entering a calculation formula

Activate the result cell then use **Table - Formula**:

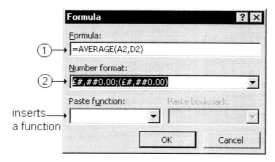

① Enter your formula, starting with an = sign.

② Select the format to apply to the result.

⇨ *Every calculation result is in fact the result of a **FIELD**. The values appear if you are viewing results, and not if you are viewing field codes.*

⇨ *To display or hide the field codes for a whole document, press $\boxed{\text{Alt}}\boxed{\text{F9}}$.
To display or hide a particular field code, place the insertion point in the field and press $\boxed{\text{⇧ Shift}}\boxed{\text{F9}}$.*

⇨ *To update the result of a calculation, place the insertion point in the field concerned and press $\boxed{\text{F9}}$.*

C-Using the application Microsoft Graph

Starting the application

▓ If the data you are going to represent are already entered in a document, copy them into the clipboard.

▓ Place the insertion point where you want to put the chart.

▓ **Insert**
Object...
double-click **Microsoft Graph 97 Chart**

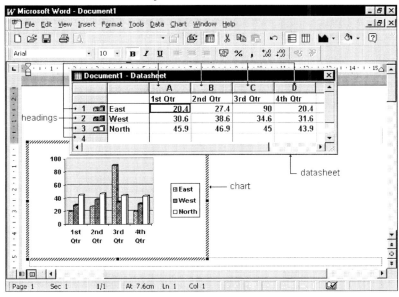

Managing the datasheet

▓ To clear the contents of cells, select the cells then use **Edit - Clear...** or press ⌊Del⌋. Choose whether you want to clear content, formatting...

▓ Enter data as you would in a Word table (you can also paste in data from the clipboard).

▓ To modify the width of one or more columns, select a cell in each column concerned then use **Format - Column Width...**

▓ To delete rows or columns, select each row or column to be deleted, by clicking its label then use **Edit - Delete** or ⌊Ctrl⌋ -.

Managing the chart

▓ To select an item in the chart, click the item.

A selected item is surrounded with handles. Drag the handles to move or resize the item.

TABLES/CHARTS

▦ To move the legend, select it then use **Format - Selected Legend - Placement** tab.

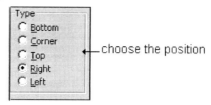

choose the position

▦ To delete the legend, select it and press ⌊Del⌋.

▦ To change the type of chart, select it then use the command **Chart - Chart Type**

▦ To specify whether the data series are in rows or columns:

Data

Series in Rows or **Series in Columns**

▦ To add an unattached text object (text box) click the chart and type the text.

▦ To add a title, use **Chart - Chart Options - Titles tab**.

▦ Enter your title.

Setting chart options

▦ To explode a pie chart slice, drag it out of the chart.

▦ To change the border, colour or shading of a bar or sector, double-click the bar or sector then activate the **Patterns** tab. Choose the effects you want to apply.

▦ To format characters, select the text item concerned then use **Format - Font...**

Leaving Microsoft Graph

▦ Click in the document outside the chart.

▦ To modify the chart, double-click it.

10.1 Forms

A-Creating a form

A form is a document containing permanent text and spaces for filling in variable data.

▪ Go into creation of a template.

▪ Enter the permanent text.

▪ Insert a form field wherever you want to collect information.

▪ Protect the completed form by clicking 🔒 or by the command **Tools - Protect Document...**.

B-Inserting form fields

A form field can be presented as a text box, a list box or a check box.

▪ Display the **Forms** toolbar.

▪ Place the insertion point where the field should appear. On the Forms toolbar, choose the type of field to insert.

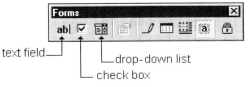

text field
check box
drop-down list

▪ Click 🖻 to define options for the field.

▪ If you are creating a list box, define each item in the list:

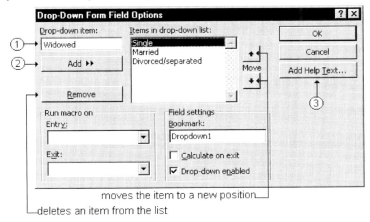

moves the item to a new position
deletes an item from the list

① Enter the item.

② Include it in the list.

③ Click here to enter a message to help the person filling in the form.

⇨ *The form fields inserted are called {FORMTEXT}, {FORMCHECKBOX}, {FORMDROPDOWN}. They can only be used if the document is protected as a form.*

C-Using a form

▧ Create a document based on the form template.

The permanent text is displayed and the fields are represented by grey areas.

▧ Move from field to field using ⇄ and ⇧ Shift ⇄ , and fill them in.

▧ When you have finished filling in the form, save it as a new document.

⇨ *You can copy the content of one text field, then paste it into another.*

⇨ *To edit a form open the template and deactivate the protection with the command* **Tools - Unprotect Document**.

D-Using a document/template with form fields

This is the type of document which is printed several times, but with a few variations each time. The type of form field you insert determines whether the items of variable data are printed and/or saved.

Creating the document/template

▧ Enter the document's permanent text.

▧ Insert **ASK** fields and/or **FILLIN** fields (use an **ASK** field if you want Word to save the data supplied by the user).

Inserting an ASK field

▧ Position the insertion point at the beginning of the document.

▧ Press Ctrl F9 .

▧ Enter the syntax for the field:
ASK space field name space "Message".

▧ At each point in the text where data input is needed, press Ctrl F9 and insert the field name.

Inserting a FILLIN field

▧ At each point in the text where data input is needed, press Ctrl F9 and enter the syntax for the field : **Fillin** space "Message".

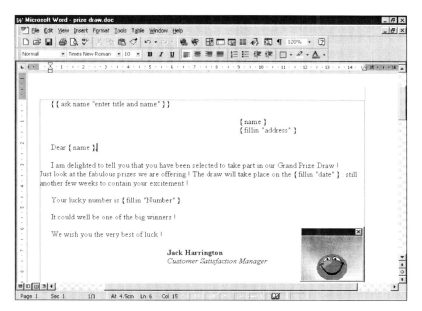

{ { ask name "enter title and name" } }

{ name }
{ fillin "address" }

Dear { name }|

I am delighted to tell you that you have been selected to take part in our Grand Prize Draw ! Just look at the fabulous prizes we are offering ! The draw will take place on the { fillin "date" } still another few weeks to contain your excitement !

Your lucky number is { fillin "Number" }

It could well be one of the big winners !

We wish you the very best of luck !

Jack Harrington
Customer Satisfaction Manager

Filling in a document/template with form fields

- Create a new document based on the template concerned, or open the document concerned.
- Select the whole document.
- Press ⌊F9⌋ to fill in the fields.

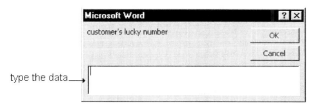

- In response to the prompt message, type in the data, pressing Enter when you need to move down to a new line. Click **OK** after each response.

⇨ *You can also fill in the form fields as the document is printing, providing that the* **Update fields** *option is active on the* **Print** *page of the* **Tools - Options** *dialog box. Wherever Word meets a field, it displays a dialog box for you to fill in the data.*

10.2 Mail merges

A-Planning a mail merge

The mail merge allows you to send out a large number of copies of a Main document to a list of addresses contained in a Data source file.

Begin by entering the permanent text of the main document, then use **Tools - Mail Merge**.

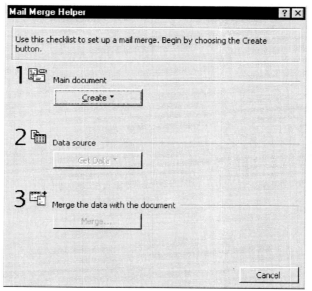

① Click the **Create** button, choose **Form Letters** then **Active Window**.

② Click the **Get Data** button then **Create Data Source** (if the data file already exists, choose **Open Data Source**).

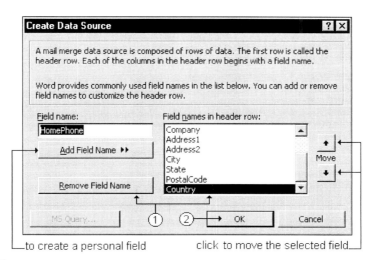

to create a personal field   click to move the selected field

① Remove each field you do not need from the **Field names in header row** list.

② Click **OK** and enter the name of the file.

▨ Click the **Edit Data Source** button and enter the data.

▨ Type in the data using ⬚ to move to the next text box and ⬚⬚ to return to the previous one. After the last line press ⬚ if you want to create another new record.

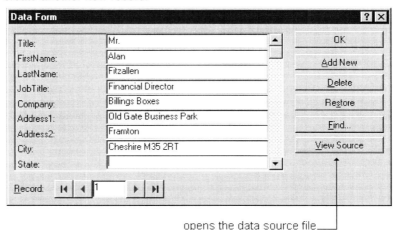

opens the data source file

▨ End by clicking the **OK** button.

In the main document, the Mail Merge toolbar appears between the ***Formatting bar*** *and the ruler:*

FORMS/MAIL MERGES

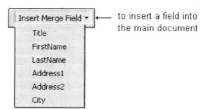

to insert a field into
the main document

Insert the fields into the permanent text.

⇨ *You can click the* [icon] *tool button to check the merge.*

B-Carrying out the mail merge

In the main document, click [icon] or [icon] to send the merge to the printer or to a new document,

C-Limiting the merge to predefined records

In the main document go into:

Tools
Mail Merge   [icon]

Click the **Merge** button.

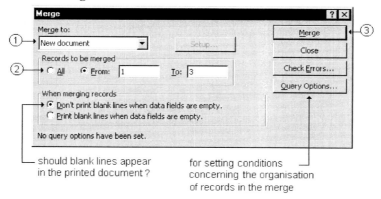

should blank lines appear
in the printed document ?

for setting conditions
concerning the organisation
of records in the merge

① Specify whether or not the merge is to go straight to the printer.

② Indicate which records are concerned.

③ Run the mail merge.

Setting out conditions for a mail merge

░ In the **Merge** dialog box, click the **Query Options** button.

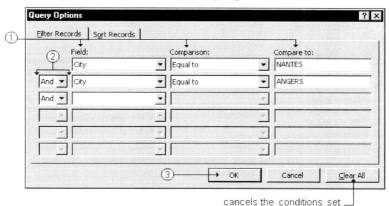

cancels the conditions set ⌐

① Set each condition.

② Choose the combination operator then set the other conditions.

③ Select the records which meet the condition.

⇨ *The conditions set are saved in the main document.*

D-Editing the data source file

░ Click to display the data form.

░ Use the form to add new records or to find records so that you can modify them or delete them.

⇨ *To change the structure of the data file, open the data file in the same way as any document. The data is entered as a table: insert columns to add new fields, or delete fields by deleting the corresponding columns.*

E-Sorting a data file

░ Open the main document.

Tools
Mail Merge

Click the **Merge** button

░ Go into the **Query Options**
Sort Records tab

FORMS/MAIL MERGES

Specify the fields by which you want to sort and the sort order associated with each.

F- Printing mailing labels

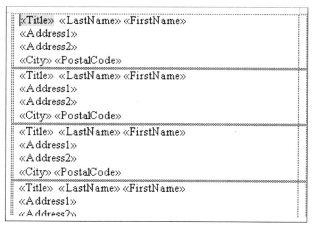

Open a new document then use **Tools - Mail Merge**.

Continue as if you were working on a letter, but instead of **Form Letters** choose **Mailing Labels**.

G-Setting conditions for printing a text

Place the insertion point where the text is to appear.

Click the **Insert Word Field** button on the Mail Merge toolbar then the **If... Then ... Else** option.

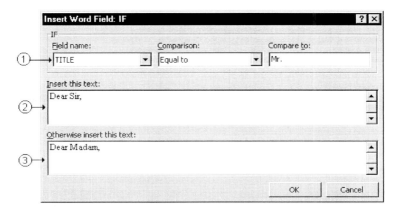

① Enter your condition.

② Enter the text which will be printed if the condition is satisfied.

③ Enter a text which will be printed if the condition is not satisfied.

H-Setting conditions for the insertion of a document

░ Place the insertion point where you wish the document to appear.

░ Insert an **IF** field, then for each action insert an INCLUDETEXT field. The syntax is:
INCLUDETEXT "File_name".

11.1 Creating and editing macros

A-Creating/running a macro

▓ Use the template concerned (**Normal.dot** is chosen by default).

▓ **Tools - Macro - Record New Macro...**

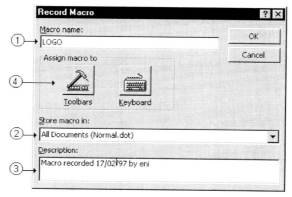

① Give the macro a name.

② Indicate where you want to save the macro.

③ Enter a **Description**.

④ Specify whether you want to run the macro by clicking a tool button or by pressing a shortcut key.

▓ If you have chosen **Toolbars** Word displays a dialog box:

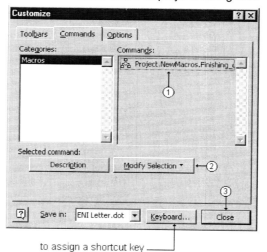

to assign a shortcut key

① Display the toolbar concerned in the Word window then drag the macro from the **Commands** list onto the bar.

② Change the look of the button on the toolbar.

③ Start to record the macro.

Go through all the actions to be memorised in the macro. When you have finished, click ▣.

To run a macro, use the tool button, or the keys that you have assigned to it.

⇨ *If you prefer to run a macro by its name, go into **Tools - Macro - Macros** or press* Alt F8 . *Word produces a list of all existing macros. Click the name of the macro you need, and then **Run**.*

B-Editing a macro

Tools - Macro - Macros... or Alt F8

In **Macro name**, choose the macro you need to modify then click the **Edit** button:

```
Sub LOGO1()

' LOGO1 Macro
' Macro recorded 17/03/97 by eni

    With Selection.ParagraphFormat
        .LeftIndent = CentimetersToPoints(5)
        .RightIndent = CentimetersToPoints(0)
        .SpaceBefore = 0
        .SpaceAfter = 0
        .LineSpacingRule = wdLineSpaceSingle
        .Alignment = wdAlignParagraphLeft
        .WidowControl = True
        .KeepWithNext = False
        .KeepTogether = False
```

Macros are written in Visual Basic.

Carry out the modifications then close the file.

C-Deleting a macro

Tools - Macro - Macros... or Alt F8

In **Macro name** choose the macro you want to delete.

Click the **Delete** button and confirm by **Yes**.

Formatting

Characters

Ctrl ⇧ Shift F	Selecting a font
Ctrl ⇧ Shift >/	
Ctrl ⇧ Shift <	Next size up/down
⇧ Shift F3	Change the case of letters
Ctrl B	Bold formatting
Ctrl ⇧ Shift H	Activate/disactivate hidden text
Ctrl	Italic formatting
Ctrl ⇧ Shift K	Format as small capitals

Ctrl U	Underline
Ctrl ⇧ Shift W	Underline individual words
Ctrl ⇧ Shift D	Double underline
Ctrl ⇧ Shift +	Superscript
Ctrl =	Subscript
Ctrl space	Normal character
Ctrl ⇧ Shift Q	Symbol font

Paragraphs

Ctrl 1/Ctrl 2	Single/Double line spacing
Ctrl 5	1.5 line spaces between lines
Ctrl 0 (zero)	Add/Delete a blank line before the paragraph
Ctrl E	Center a paragraph
Ctrl L	Left Align

Ctrl R	Right Align
Ctrl J	Justify a paragraph
Ctrl ⇧ Shift M	Increase/decrease left indent
Ctrl T/	
Ctrl ⇧ Shift T	Increase/decrease hanging indent of first line
Ctrl Q	Standard Paragraph

Various

Ctrl ⇧ Shift N	Return to Normal style
Ctrl ⇧ Shift C	Copy formatting
Ctrl ⇧ Shift V	Paste formatting

Alt Ctrl K	Run autoformat
Alt Ctrl 1	
Alt Ctrl 2	Apply style (Heading1, Heading2, Heading3)
Alt Ctrl 3	

Moving/selecting/entering text

Ctrl ←	Delete the word to the left of the insertion point
Ctrl Del	Delete the word to the righ of the insertion
Ins	Overwrite/insertion modes

Moving

Key	Action
↓/↑	Following/preceding line
→/←	Following/preceding character
End /Home	End/beginning of a line
Pg Up /Pg Dn	Previous/following screen paragraph

Key	Action
Ctrl Home / Ctrl End	Beginning/ end of the document
Ctrl Alt Pg Up / Ctrl Alt Pg Dn	Top/bottom of the window
Ctrl ↑ / Ctrl ↓	Previous/following

Selecting

F8	Select text
Ctrl ⇧ Shift F8	Select columns
⇧ Shift F8	Return to previous selection
Ctrl A	Select whole document

Inserting symbols and variable data

⇧ Shift Enter	Line break
Ctrl Enter	Page break
Ctrl ⇧ Shift Enter	Column break
Ctrl -	Conditional hyphen
F3	Insert AutoText entry
Alt ⇧ Shift T	Insert time field
Alt ⇧ Shift D	Insert date field

Key	Action
Alt ⇧ Shift P	Insert page field
Ctrl Alt C	Copyright symbol
Ctrl Alt R	Registered Trademark symbol
Ctrl Alt T	Trademark symbol
Ctrl _	Nonbreaking hyphen
Ctrl ⇧ Shift space	Nonbreaking space

SPECIFIC SHORTCUT KEYS

Fields

F9	Update selected field
Ctrl F9	Insert a field

Key	Action
⇧ Shift F9 / Alt F9	Display/hide a selected field code/all field codes

Tables

⇄ /	Select next cell
⇧ Shift ⇄	Select previous cell
Alt 5	Select whole table

Key	Action
Alt End	Go to the last cell of the row
Alt Home	Go to the first cell of the row
Alt Pg Dn / Alt Pg Up	Go to the last/ first cell of the column

APPENDIX

Outlines

Alt + ⇧ Shift + ←	Level +1
Alt + ⇧ Shift + →	Level -1
Alt	
⇧ Shift **1 à 9**	Display by heading level
Alt + ⇧ Shift +	Develop a heading
Alt + ⇧ Shift -	Reduce a heading
Alt + ⇧ Shift **A**	Display whole document (heading, Sub-heading, texts)

Alt + ⇧ Shift ↑	Move a heading towards the one before
Alt + ⇧ Shift ↓	Move a heading towards the one after
Ctrl + ⇧ Shift F6	Activate the last window

Mail Merges

Alt + ⇧ Shift **N**	Merge to a new document
Alt + ⇧ Shift **M**	Print a merged document

Alt + ⇧ Shift **E**	Modify the data file

MENU SHORTCUT KEYS

File

Ctrl **N**	New...
Ctrl **O**	Open...
Ctrl **W**	Close
Ctrl **S**	Save
Ctrl **P**	Print...
Alt F4	Exit
Ctrl F2	Print preview

Edit

Ctrl **Z**	Undo
Ctrl **Y**	Repeat
Ctrl **X**	Cut
Ctrl **C**	Copy
Ctrl **V**	Paste
Ctrl **A**	Select All
Ctrl **G**	Go To ...
Ctrl **F**	Find
Ctrl **H**	Replace

View

Ctrl + Alt **N**	Normal
Ctrl + Alt **O**	Outline
Ctrl + Alt **P**	Page Layout

Insert

Ctrl + Alt **F**	Footnote
Ctrl + Alt **E**	Endnote
Alt + ⇧ Shift **X**	Mark index entry
Ctrl **K**	Hyperlink

Format

`Ctrl` **D**	Font...
`Alt` `Ctrl` **K**	AutoFormat... Tools
`⇧ Shift` `F7`	Thesaurus...
`F7`	Spelling check
`Alt` `F8`	Macros
`Alt` `F11`	Visual Basic Editor

Table

`Alt` **5**	Select table

APPENDIX

VARIOUS SHORTCUT KEYS

`⇧ Shift` `F10`	Displays a context-sensitive menu
`⇧ Shift` `F5`	Return to last three positions
`⇧ Shift` `F4`	Reruns a search
`⇧ Shift` `F2` /	Copy/
`F2`	move text without using clipboard
`F6` / `⇧ Shift` `F6`	Move to next/previous pane
`Ctrl` `⇧ Shift` *	Display non-printing characters
`F1` / `⇧ Shift` `F1`	Summary of Help/On line Help

Microsoft Word 97

!

A

AUTOTEXT

B

BACKGROUND

See also COLOUR

BOOKMARK

BREAK

C

CALCULATIONS

See also FIELDS, TABLES

CHARACTERS

See also FORMATTING, EDITING TEXT, ENTERING TEXT

CHARTS

COLOUR

COLUMNS

See also TABLES

COPYING/MOVING

See also MOVING AROUND

D

DATE

DELETING

DOCUMENT

DRAWING

E

EDITING TEXT

ENTERING TEXT

ENVELOPE

F

FIELDS

FILL EFFECTS

FINDING/REPLACING

INDEX

G

GRAMMAR

H

HEADER

See PAGE SETUP

HYPERLINK

HYPHENATION

I

INDEX

See TABLES

L

LINE

M

MAIL MERGE

MARGIN

See also PAGE SETUP

MASTER DOCUMENTS

MOVING

See COPYING/MOVING

MOVING AROUND

N

NOTES

NUMBERS

See also FIELDS, TABLES

O

OBJECTS

See also DRAWING, PICTURE, SOUND, VIDEO

OFFICE ASSISTANT

OUTLINE

P

PAGE

See also PAGE SETUP

INDEX

INDEX

WINDOW

WORDART

ZOOM

ENI
Publishing

▲ **Quick Reference Guide**
▲ **User Manual**
▲ **Practical Guide**
▲ **Training CD-ROM**
▲ **Microsoft®**
   Approved Publication

**Ask for
our free brochure**

**For more information
on our new titles
please complete
this card and return**

Name: ....

....

Company: ....

Address: ....

....

Postcode: ....

Town: ....

Phone: ....

E-mail: ....

Please
affix
stamp
here

ENI Publishing LTD

500 Chiswick High Road

London W4 5RG